YOUNG SCIENTIST CONCEPTS & PROJECTS

THE BODY

STEVE PARKER

Gareth Stevens Publishing
MILWAUKEE

**For a free color catalog describing
Gareth Stevens' list of high-quality
books and multimedia programs,
call 1-800-542-2595 (USA) or 1-800-461-9120
(Canada). Gareth Stevens Publishing's Fax:
(414) 225-0377. See our catalog, too, on the
World Wide Web: http://gsinc.com**

Library of Congress Cataloging-in-Publication Data

Parker, Steve.
The body / by Steve Parker.
p. cm. — (Young scientist concepts and projects)
Includes bibliographical references and index.
Summary: Describes the different parts of the body and
uses activities and experiments to help explain how
they do what they are supposed to do.
ISBN 0-8368-2084-3 (lib. bdg.)
1. Human physiology—Juvenile literature. 2. Body,
Human—Juvenile literature. [1. Body, Human. 2. Human
physiology.] I. Title. II. Series.
QP37.P268   1998
612—dc21   97-41627

This North American edition first published in 1998 by
Gareth Stevens Publishing
1555 North RiverCenter Drive, Suite 201
Milwaukee, WI 53212 USA

Original edition © 1996 by Anness Publishing Limited.
First published in 1996 by Lorenz Books, an imprint of Anness Publishing Inc.,
New York, New York. This U.S. edition © 1998 by Gareth Stevens, Inc.
Additional end matter © 1998 by Gareth Stevens, Inc.

Senior Editor: Caroline Beattie
Photographer: John Freeman
Stylist: Thomasina Smith
Designer: Caroline Reeves
Picture Researcher: Liz Eddison
Illustrator: Alisa Tingley
Gareth Stevens series editor: Dorothy L. Gibbs
Editorial assistant: Diane Laska

Printed in the United States of America

1 2 3 4 5 6 7 8 9 02 01 00 99 98

THE BODY

CONTENTS

YOUR BODY

The body has a strong framework of bones to hold it up. There are more than 200 bones and hundreds of other parts inside the human body.

What do you see most each day? Schoolwork? Or television? Many of us spend time each day people watching – looking at human bodies belonging to friends, relatives, teachers, store owners, and many others. We watch these bodies move, walk, talk, eat, laugh, cry, and carry out their daily lives. You probably know a lot about the people you see every day. But how much do you know about the human body itself? Why does the body have two arms and two legs, with the head on top? Why does it have hair and fingernails? What makes it run, jump, and speak? What happens to food after it is swallowed? And how does the body work on the inside?

Our bodies change throughout our lives. As children age, they grow bigger. As adults grow older, they may shrink slightly. Can you remember how small you were, and how big and tall everyone else seemed when you were younger? What are your earliest memories?

Different types

There are two main kinds of human bodies — male and female. The female ones are called girls when young and women when grown up. The male ones are called boys when young and men when grown up.

Different shapes

Bodies vary on the outside, even when they are all the same age. Some are taller than others. Some have different colored hair, eyes, and skin than others. But, on the inside, bodies are all much the same.

Sometimes the body needs to eat. Food gives it energy and nutrients for moving around, growing, and carrying out all its life processes.

Sometimes the body stays still. It can be standing, sitting, or lying down when it does this. Yet, inside, parts like the heart are still moving.

Sometimes the body does active things, like running. It can jog slowly or sprint fast, and kick or throw a ball at the same time!

This book answers all these questions and many more. It shows how your eyes work, what your bones look like, how your heart beats, and what happens in your brain. Learning about the body is easy, because you always have one to study!

Sometimes the body rests and sleeps. Every body needs to sleep, usually at night. Younger bodies generally need more sleep than older ones.

FACT BOX

• Each human body is a member of the animal group, or species, that scientists call *Homo sapiens* ("Wise Human").

• There are about 6 billion human bodies in the world. By the year 2050, it is estimated there will be 12 billion of us.

• No animals have spread to as many places in the world as people. We live in snowy polar lands, in tropical forests, in arid deserts, and on high mountains. After us, the next most widespread animal is the field mouse.

Sometimes the body does quiet things, like reading, listening to music, drawing pictures, or solving puzzles. It can learn lots of new skills and information at this time.

MEASURE YOUR BODY

To measure your weight, simply stand on a scale. Take off your shoes and heavy clothing, like your coat and sweater, since these make you seem heavier. Don't worry about light clothing like T-shirts. Note your weight in pounds (kilograms).

How tall are you? How much do you weigh? What size shoes do you wear? You may know the answers to these questions – or you can find out by measuring. But what about your hat, collar, or glove size? We measure the body to find out its size and shape for many reasons. A doctor measures the weight of a new baby to make sure it is healthy and growing well. An optician measures a person's eyes for glasses. A tailor measures neck, waist, chest, arms, and legs to make clothes that fit well. How do you measure up?

MATERIALS

You will need: tape measure, large roll of paper (such as the back of a roll of unwanted wallpaper), colored pens.

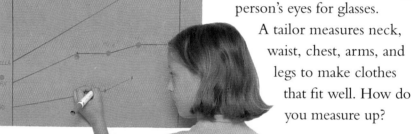

Draw a graph of your body measurements over months, or even years.

Measure parts of your body

1 Measure around the waist at the level where you'd wear a belt.

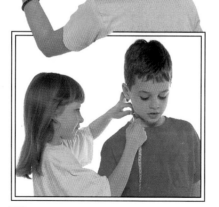

2 Measure around the neck at its narrowest point.

3 Measure the arm from the point of the shoulder to the wrist.

Make a chart of your body's different measurements over the years. Use different colors for height, weight, waist size, and so on. Measure yourself at regular times, such as every three months, or on your birthday, or on the last day of each school year. Which measurement changes most, and which changes least?

Same age, different size

Get together with some friends of the same age. How much variation is there between all of you in height or weight? Try the same test on children who are much younger, such as two years old. Do the same for grown-ups who are 20 years old. Which age has the most variation?

Body outline
Have a friend outline your body with colored pen on a large roll of paper. Date the outline. Outline your friend, using a different color. Who's grown the most?

Feet and hands
Have your friend draw carefully around your foot and hand. Do the same for your friend. Who has the thinnest fingers, the widest palm, or the thickest wrist?

FACES

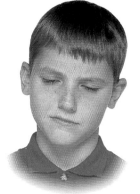

Face paints or cosmetic makeup can alter a face completely. You can become a funny clown, a wizened witch, or a movie star. Makeup also helps with acting and pretending. If it makes you look like an animal, such as a cat or mouse, you may find it easier to act like that animal.

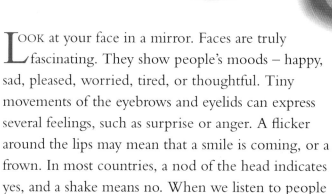

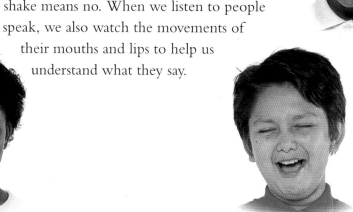

Look at your face in a mirror. Faces are truly fascinating. They show people's moods – happy, sad, pleased, worried, tired, or thoughtful. Tiny movements of the eyebrows and eyelids can express several feelings, such as surprise or anger. A flicker around the lips may mean that a smile is coming, or a frown. In most countries, a nod of the head indicates yes, and a shake means no. When we listen to people speak, we also watch the movements of their mouths and lips to help us understand what they say.

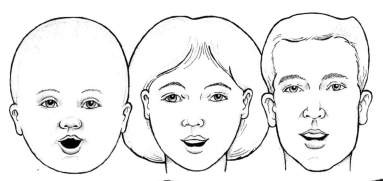

How faces change with age

As you grow, your face gets bigger. It also changes its proportions. A baby's face is small compared to the size of its whole head. Its eyes and forehead are big. Its nose and mouth are small. On a grown-up, the nose and mouth take up more of the face, and the face takes up more than half of the front of the head.

Two-sided face

Both sides of a face seem the same. They could be perfect mirror images of each other. But are they exactly identical – that is, are they symmetrical? Here is a normal photograph of a boy's face. Compare it with the following photographs.

Two right sides

The left side of the face in this photograph has been replaced with a reversed version of the right side. So this face is the boy's right half plus a mirror image of it. Does it look like the real face shown in the photograph on the left?

Two left sides

The right side of the face in this photograph has been replaced with a reversed version of the left side. So this face is the boy's left half plus a mirror-image of it. Does it look more like the real face than the two-right-sides face in the middle?

Young and old

A baby's face usually has smooth, soft skin. After many years, human skin may develop wrinkles and lines. This is entirely natural. It is more likely to happen if the person spends a lot of time in the sun and wind.

FACT BOX

• Most grown-ups can recognize at least 500 people from their faces. This includes family and friends, as well as famous faces from the worlds of music, movies, and sports.

• When you see your face in a mirror, it is not the face that other people see. It is reversed, left to right. This is why some people are surprised by the way they look in photographs.

• To see yourself as others see you, study a photograph of yourself. Compare it with your face in a mirror. Which one do you like best? Is it the most familiar one?

Disguise

To disguise yourself, start with your face, which is the part of your body that other people recognize most. You could wear a large hat and glasses, or take off glasses you usually wear. A beard or a mustache and a scarf might help. The more of your face you cover up, the less recognizable you are.

SKIN, HAIR, AND NAILS

Hair, like skin, keeps growing. Most people have about 100,000 hairs on their heads. Each hair grows for a couple of years. It could reach more than a yard (meter) in length. Then, it usually falls out, and a new hair grows in.

THE body is covered with skin – well, not quite. There are openings for parts such as the eyes, ears, nose, and mouth, but the rest is skin. This body covering is flexible and stretchy, so you can move. It keeps body fluids and other substances inside. It keeps germs, dirt, and other substances outside. Skin always is being worn away as you move around, get washed and dressed, and grip and hold objects. But new skin always is growing just under the surface, to replace the skin that is worn away. Most of the skin over the body is covered with hair. Some of these hairs are thick and easily seen, like the hairs on your head.

Other hairs are so small that you need a magnifying glass to see them. Only a few parts of the body are truly hairless, like the palms of the hands and soles of the feet.

With a magnifying glass, look very closely at the skin on different parts of your body. See how it varies. Some parts are smooth and flat. Others have lines and creases, especially around joints, where the skin stretches and bends a lot.

Handy skin
A hand has different kinds of skin – smooth, creased, thick, thin, hairless, and hairy, as well as nails. Skin, hair, and nails all are made from the substance called keratin. This is the same stuff that makes up the claws, hooves, and horns of some animals.

Close to skin
Under a powerful microscope, even the smoothest skin has tiny hills and valleys, lines and creases. Sweat oozes up through tiny dotlike holes, called sweat pores.

Even closer to skin
Individual flakes of skin are microscopic dead cells, flattened and filled with tough keratin. They fall off the body by the thousands every minute.

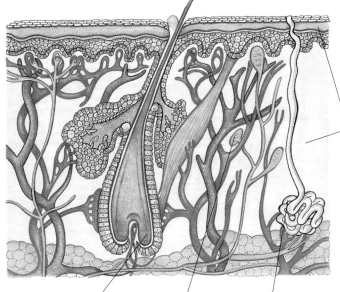

Hair root / Touch sensor / Sweat gland

Giant hair

When you get this close to a hair, it does not look so smooth and shiny! The whole hair is dead, except for its very lowest part, the root, under the skin's surface.

Epidermis

Dermis

Inside skin

Skin has two layers. The upper layer is the epidermis. This layer keeps growing to replace flakes of skin that are worn away. The lower layer is the dermis. It has tiny touch sensors, nerves, and blood vessels.

Skin color

Different colors of skin and hair are due to different amounts of the very dark pigment (coloring substance) called melanin. Small patches of skin with slightly more melanin than surrounding skin are called freckles.

FACT BOX

• If the skin of an adult human could be spread out flat, it would cover 21 square feet (2 square meters).

• The thickest skin is on the soles of the feet. If you do not wear shoes, it grows even thicker, possibly to more than 1/4 inch (6 millimeters) thick.

• The thinnest skin, on the eyelids, is less than two-hundredths of an inch (0.5 mm).

• An average hair grows about 0.04 inch (1 mm) every three days. An average fingernail grows about the same amount every seven days.

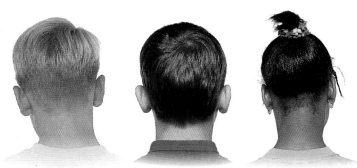

Hair types

Hair can be dark or light, thick (coarse) or thin (fine), and straight, wavy, or curly. The length of the hair and the way it is styled greatly alter its appearance.

TOUCH AND FEELING

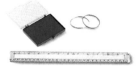

You will need: 2 pencils with sharp points, ruler, 2 rubber bands, ink pad, strips of pale paper or cardboard, magnifying glass.

WHEN you touch an object, your skin tells you many things about it. You can feel whether it is hard or soft, hot or cold, rough or smooth, wet or dry. Touch comes from millions of microscopic sensors all over your skin. These sensors detect light contact and heavy pressure, movement, temperature, and other features. They send nerve signals to your brain, telling you what you are feeling. However, the touch sensors are not spread evenly all over the body. Some areas of skin have more of them, so they are more sensitive than other areas. Fingertips, with their swirly ridges, are very sensitive to the slightest touch.

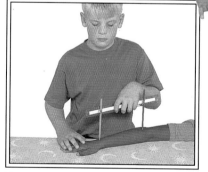

Sensitive points

1 Fasten the pencils to the ruler with the rubber bands, *as shown.* Line up one pencil point with the 0 on the ruler. Leave a wide gap.

2 Ask a friend to close his/her eyes. Gently touch his/her arm with both pencil points. Does your friend feel two points or one?

3 Reduce the gap between the pencils and touch your friend's arm again. The most sensitive skin will detect even the smallest gap.

Stamping fingerprints

1 Swirly skin-ridge patterns on the fingers are called fingerprints. To see them, press your finger or thumb on an ink pad with a rolling motion.

2 With the same rolling motion, press your finger or thumb onto a strip of paper or cardboard to transfer the ink and make a print.

3 Make prints for all of your fingers and both thumbs, and label them. Ask some friends to make their own set of fingerprints, too.

Studying fingerprints

Study the sets of fingerprints carefully under a magnifying glass. See how they have various patterns. These patterns are called whorls (which are like part-spirals), arches, and loops. With practice, you can recognize your own prints. Are the prints of your family members similar to your own?

Every print is different

No two people in the whole world have the same fingerprints. We all have different print patterns. This is why fingerprints can be used to prove that a person has been at a certain place. When fingers touch a surface, they leave tiny traces of natural skin oil and sweat in the same pattern as the prints. A special powder dusted over them reveals the pattern.

13

EYES AND SIGHT

THE body has five main senses that receive information about its surroundings. They are touch, sight, hearing, smell, and taste. About half of the total knowledge and memory in the brain gets there through the eyes. This happens when you read words and look at pictures and diagrams, as you are doing now, and when you see people, objects, and scenes around you. The eyes detect colors and patterns of light rays, turn them into nerve signals, and send them to the brain. Since vision is so important, everyone should have an eye test every year or two. (People who are blind or cannot see clearly rely more on other senses, like hearing and touch.)

The eyes have their own small lenses to focus light rays for a clear view. Extra lenses like those in binoculars make things look larger and nearer.

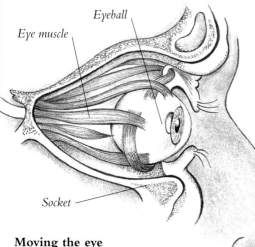

Eyeball

Eye muscle

Socket

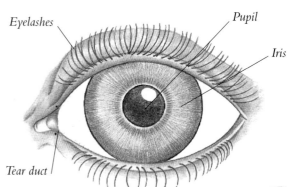

Eyelashes

Pupil

Iris

Tear duct

Moving the eye

The eyeball sits snugly in the bowl-shaped skull bone called a socket, or orbit. Six small muscles join each eyeball to the bone behind it. They pull the eyeball in different ways to make it twist and swivel. This is how you look up, down, and to each side.

Look into my eyes …

Most of the eyeball is behind skin and skull bone, inside the head. The dark spot in the center is the pupil, where light goes into the eye. Eyelashes keep dust off the eye's sensitive front surface. Eyelids blink to wipe tear fluid over the eye and wash away dirt and germs.

Inside the eye

The cutaway view *(below)* shows the small and delicate parts inside the eyeball. Light comes in through the clear dome-shaped cornea at the front and passes through the pupil, the circular hole in the iris. The light rays are focused (bent), so they shine a clear, sharp image onto the back of the eye. This area is lined by the retina, which contains millions of light-sensitive cells. When the cells receive light rays, they create nerve signals which pass along the optic nerve to the brain.

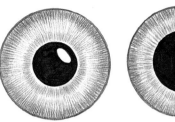  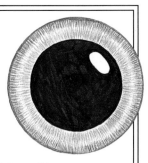

Iris and pupil

The eye's inside is very sensitive. Too much light is harmful. So the pupil gets smaller in bright light to prevent maximum light. It widens in dim light, to see better. This happens by a change in the size of the iris, the colored ring of muscle around the pupil.

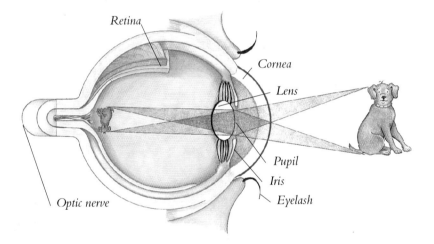

Retina

Cornea

Lens

Pupil

Iris

Eyelash

Optic nerve

Eye care

Eyes can be harmed by dust, splashes of chemicals, objects like thrown stones or flying insects, and too much light – including bright sunshine. It is always wise to protect your eyes with goggles or sunglasses.

Eye color

Eye color refers to the color of the iris. It may be brown, green, blue, gray, or nearly black. Newborns have blue eyes. The color usually changes after several months.

TRICKING THE EYES

E YES cannot see everything, all around, all the time. When you look straight at something, to see its details, you miss what goes on around the sides. Also, illusions and movements occur in daily life that trick the eye. These illusions fool the eye – or actually, they fool the brain. It is the brain that analyzes the nerve signals from the eyes, identifies objects and colors and movements, and understands what you see.

You will need: a compass, white cardboard, colored pencils and marker, scissors, toothpicks.

This picture shows a white triangle – or does it? There seems to be a solid white triangle blocking out parts of the black circles and black triangle. The brain actually imagines the white triangle.

Optical illusions trick the brain. On one side, this figure (right) looks like three round tubes. But, on the other side, it looks like two square tubes. The pattern of lines on paper creates a puzzling picture.

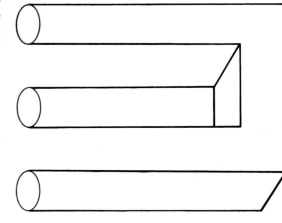

Hole-in-the-head?

If the brain cannot understand all of a scene, it makes up hidden parts and fills the gaps. Do that here, and the boy has an arrow through his head. But common sense tells us it is a trick. Sure enough, the arrow parts are joined by a curved piece of wire hidden in the boy's hair.

Spiral spinner

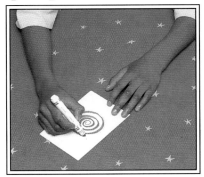

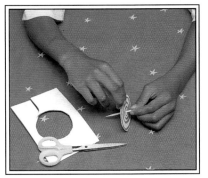

1 Use a compass to draw a 6-inch (15-centimeter) circle on a piece of cardboard. Then draw a spiral shape, *as shown*. Use a pencil first to get the right shape, then color it.

2 Carefully cut around the circle's edge to make a disk with the spiral on it. Push a toothpick through the disk's center, making sure the toothpick is a tight fit.

3 Spin the disk like a toy top. One way, the spiral seems to move inward and disappear into the toothpick. The other way, it seems to move out and fall off the disk's edge. Of course, it really goes nowhere!

Moving circles

Color wheel

1 Draw several spirals or circles on a piece of cardboard. Make them clear and colorful. On another piece of cardboard, draw more spirals and circles. Hold one piece of cardboard still, and move the other in small circles.

2 Can you make sense of what you see? Do the circles seem to rotate? This is a very unusual scene that the brain has trouble understanding. What effect do you see if you move both pieces of cardboard in small circles?

1 For a color wheel, divide a 4-inch (10-cm) disk of cardboard into seven equal slices or segments. Color in the segments like a rainbow, with the colors of the spectrum in the correct order: red, orange, yellow, green, blue, indigo, violet.

2 Push a toothpick through the center of the disk and spin it fast. The colors merge into white or, perhaps, gray, because white light is a mixture of many different colors of light (the spectrum). The spinning wheel merges these colors to form white.

EARS AND HEARING

LISTEN carefully. What can you hear? Even in the quietest place, there are sounds – whistling wind, rustling leaves, singing birds, a car, or a plane. Hearing is the body sense that detects sound waves. Sound waves are invisible "ripples" that come from any object making a noise, whether it is a cat "purrrrrrring" or a stereo pounding out music. The ripples are vibrations, or fast back-and-forth movements, of the tiny floating molecules that make up air. Vibrations pass through air into your ears. The inner parts of the ears detect the vibrations and change them into nerve signals, which go to the brain. Parts of the inner ears called semi-circular canals also help you sense movements and gravity, to help you keep your balance.

Protect your ears from extreme cold, loud sounds, or very dusty air. Like eyes, ears are delicate and easily harmed. Never push or poke anything into the ear canal. It should keep itself clean naturally.

Ear shapes
What we call the "ear" has little to do with hearing. It is simply a curved flap of skin and cartilage on the side of the head. Ears come in many shapes and sizes, but this has little effect on hearing. Ears gather sound waves and funnel them into the inner ear canal.

On the phone
When you listen on the telephone, sound waves go from the earpiece straight down the outer ear canal. This canal is about $1^1/_4$ inches (3 cm) long. A thin piece of skin, called the eardrum *(shown on the next page)*, is stretched across the end of the canal. It is about the size of your fingernail. Sound waves bounce off the eardrum and make it vibrate.

18

A doctor looks into the ear with an otoscope to check for infections or other problems. The eardrum looks like a patch of thin reddish skin with the hammer bone just behind it.

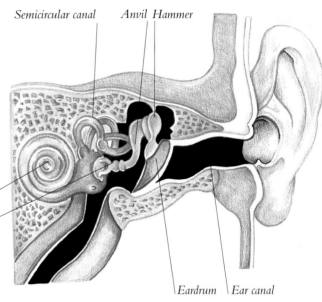

Semicircular canal   Anvil Hammer

Cochlea

Stirrup

Eardrum   Ear canal

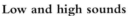

Low and high sounds

Some sounds are deep and booming, like thunder or a big drum. Others are high and shrill, like squealing tires or a cymbal. Difference in sounds is called pitch or frequency, and it is measured in Hertz (Hz). Human ears hear many frequencies, from the deepest notes at 25 Hz to extremely high ones at 15,000 Hz. In general, when big objects vibrate, they make deeper sounds. A large hand bell has a lower sound or musical note than a small hand bell. Some animals can hear ultrasounds, like the squeaks of bats, which are sounds too high pitched for human ears to detect.

Inside the ear

Sound vibrations hit the eardrum and pass along three tiny bones, the hammer, anvil, and stirrup, to fluid inside the snail-shaped cochlea. Here, the vibrations are turned into nerve signals that move along the cochlear nerve to the brain.

Not too loud

The loudness of a sound is called its volume. It is measured in decibels. Sounds louder than about 85 to 90 decibels can damage the delicate inner parts of the ear, especially if they go on for a long time. Loud sounds from earphones or speakers can harm your hearing. People who work near noisy machines, such as road drills and airplanes, wear earplugs to cut down the volume and protect their hearing.

LOUD AND QUIET

Whis you hear a very loud noise, like a banging drum, do you turn away and put your hands over your ears? And, when you try to hear something very quiet, like a whisper, do you lean forward and turn one ear toward it? Your body's position and movements help you hear and keep your ears from being damaged by loud noises. Here are some projects that show you how to make sounds seem louder and how to see the vibrations of sound waves. The megaphone *(below)* is a funnel shape which, like an extra-big mouth, collects sound waves from your voice and makes them spread forward only. A megaphone also works the other way around, like an extra-big ear, called an ear trumpet, which collects lots of sound waves.

Drums are fun but loud. The harder you hit them, the more the drum head (skin) vibrates and the louder the sound. Bigger drums make lower, deeper sounds.

Whispers are quiet and, usually, secret. If there are other sounds, like people talking or music playing, you may have to get very close to the whisperer to hear.

Megaphone

1 Carefully cut out this shape from a large sheet of thin cardboard. When rolled up and taped, it will form a funnel shape, which can be a megaphone or an ear trumpet.

2 Roll the cardboard into a funnel or cone shape. Make the big end as wide as possible and the small end about 1¹/₂ inches (4 cm) across. Tape the funnel to hold this shape.

3 Listen normally to a friend talk. Then listen with the funnel as an ear trumpet. Talk to a friend normally. Then talk through the megaphone. Does the sound change?

Copy your ear

1 Cover one side of the pan with a sheet of plastic wrap. Make sure the plastic wrap is stretched tightly across with no creases. If necessary, fasten it to the pan with tape.

2 Push the short end of one straw into the long end of another. Carefully cut a few slits in the remaining long end so it spreads out, to hold the ball.

3 Tape the Ping-Pong ball onto the folded-back slits in the straw. Bend the straws at right angles and secure with tape. Tape the other straw to the plastic wrap, *as shown*.

The sheet of plastic wrap works like your ear-drum. It vibrates when sound waves hit it.

The straw works like your tiny ear bones. It passes vibrations along to the next part.

The bowl of water is like your cochlea. Vibrations spread as ripples across it.

MATERIALS

You will need: a pan without a base (like a springform baking pan), plastic wrap, tape, 2 flexible plastic drinking straws, scissors, Ping-Pong ball, bowl of water.

4 Rest the pan, on its side, on another bowl or on some books. Bend the straws and position them so the ball just touches the water in the bowl. This setup is like your ear! Create some sound waves near the pan, by clapping, for instance. The sound waves hit the plastic wrap, which is like your eardrum, and make it vibrate. The vibrations travel along the straws, which work like the tiny ear bones, to the ball, making ripples in the bowl of water, which is like the fluid-filled cochlea. As a result, you can "see" sound waves.

NOSE AND SMELL

CAN you remember scents and smells for a long time? Perhaps you recall the smell of a holiday dinner table or a relative's house. Smell is one of the body's five main senses. The smell area inside the nose detects tiny invisible particles, called odor molecules, floating in the air. Smell determines if foods and drinks are bad or rotten. It also warns us of danger, such as the nose-wrinkling stench of stagnant, polluted water. Smell also provides pleasure, such as the lovely scents of flowers and candles and the aromas of good food.

Enjoy the scents of the beautiful blooms. Sniff each type of flower, in turn, and ask your friends which scent they like best. People have different personal preferences for scents and odors.

Your nose runs or gets blocked when you have an infection caused by germs, such as a cold. Get rid of the nasal mucus by blowing into a tissue or a handkerchief.

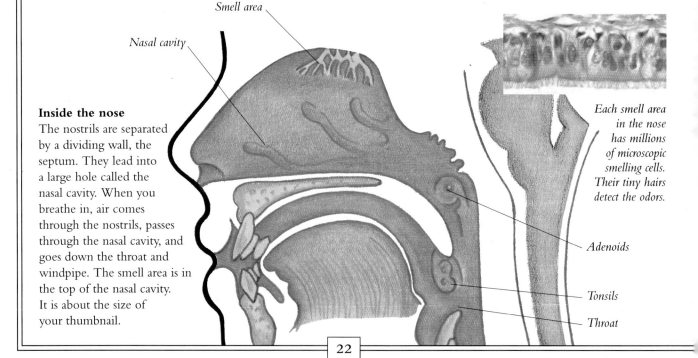

Inside the nose

The nostrils are separated by a dividing wall, the septum. They lead into a large hole called the nasal cavity. When you breathe in, air comes through the nostrils, passes through the nasal cavity, and goes down the throat and windpipe. The smell area is in the top of the nasal cavity. It is about the size of your thumbnail.

Smell area

Nasal cavity

Each smell area in the nose has millions of microscopic smelling cells. Their tiny hairs detect the odors.

Adenoids

Tonsils

Throat

A mouth-watering meal

Would you eat this delicious-smelling meal? Smell alone can make you hungry. Your brain recognizes food smells and gets your body ready. Watery saliva comes into your mouth, ready to moisten the food. This is why good foods smell "mouth watering."

Old and rotten

Would you eat this old, rotting food? It looks awful, and, if you could smell it, that would be even worse! If foods or drinks smell bad or rotten, they might cause food poisoning. So, we avoid them. Smell gives us an early warning before we taste. This warning is an important use of the sense of smell.

Overpowering fragrance

A few flowers are fine, but a whole field can be overpowering. Some smells are pleasant in normal amounts, but, if they are too strong, they are not so nice. The amount or concentration of a smell alters its effect on us.

Sniff, sniff ...

Is that smoke? This odor warns us at once about the presence of fire. The body becomes ready for action. Animals react in the same way to the smell of a forest fire.

FACT BOX

• Most people could identify at least 10,000 different smells, if they had the time to try them all.

• A bloodhound can pick up scents at least 1,000 times better than a person.

• The smell areas inside the top of the nose have 20 million smelling cells.

TONGUE AND TASTE

Many animals use their tongues to clean their faces, whiskers, paws, and other body parts. People do not need to, since we have hands, soap, and water. But, sometimes, you might lick a stray bit of food or drink from your lips, or even your nose – if you can reach it!

AS you eat a meal, you probably lick your lips slightly to clean them. Licking your lips also moistens them, so they seal together well and stop food and drink from dribbling out. Your tongue does many other jobs, too. It provides your sense of taste by detecting tiny particles called flavor molecules in foods and drinks. Along with smell, taste helps you determine if foods are sour, rotten, or bad and should not be eaten. The tongue moves food around in your mouth, so you can chew it properly. It also helps you talk clearly by moving around as you speak and make other sounds.

Examine your tongue in a mirror. Do you see your tongue's rough surface and the lumps (papillae)?

Bumpy tongue

The top surface of the tongue is covered with small bumps called papillae *(right)*. There are different kinds of papillae. The larger ones are at the back. All the papillae help to grip food as you bite and chew.

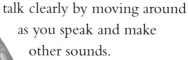

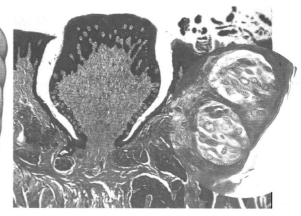

Taste buds

The photograph *(above)* shows an enlarged, cut-through view of one papilla. Set into its lower edges (the stalk) are tiny taste buds. The view *at the right* shows two taste buds with their tasting cells.

Flavors on the tongue

There are four main tastes – sweet, salty, sour, and bitter. All food flavors are combinations of these four. They are detected on different parts of the tongue, as shown on this "taste map" *(left)*. The middle of the tongue tastes almost nothing at all. There are also some taste buds on the roof of the mouth and in the upper throat.

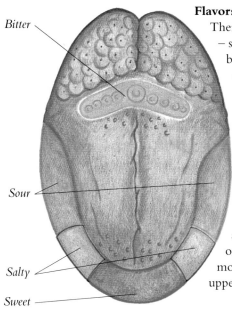

Bitter

Sour

Salty

Sweet

Favorite flavors

Favorite tastes differ from one person to another. Most babies and young people like sweet foods. Some older people prefer salty, spicy, or sour tastes. Firmness and texture are also important. Some foods seem slimy, slippery, or lumpy. Which of these foods do you like?

FACT BOX

• A typical tongue has more than 8,000 taste buds on it.

• Each taste bud has 20 to 30 "tasting cells" that detect flavors.

• A tasting cell in a taste bud lives only 10 days. Then, it dies, but it is replaced within 12 hours by another one.

• Babies have more taste buds than adults, perhaps as many as 10,000.

• Older people usually have fewer taste buds, perhaps 5,000. They may say that foods are bland and tasteless – younger people with more taste buds disagree!

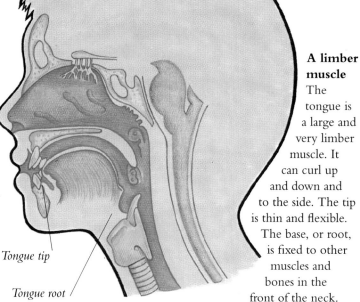

Tongue tip

Tongue root

A limber muscle

The tongue is a large and very limber muscle. It can curl up and down and to the side. The tip is thin and flexible. The base, or root, is fixed to other muscles and bones in the front of the neck.

SMELL OR TASTE?

Some smells are similar. Sniff a spoonful of honey, then some jam. Can you tell the difference? They both smell sweet. Perhaps the jam has fruits in it, or the honey has real honeycomb.

W HEN you eat and drink, you use the senses of taste, smell, touch, and sight – all together! You detect flavors using the taste buds on your tongue. You detect odors that float from the back of your mouth up into the back of your nose as you chew. You assess the temperature, firmness, moistness, and texture of food with the different types of touch sensors in your mouth. This is different from taste. You also look at the food with your eyes to get an impression of how it might taste. All four of these senses tell you about the odors and flavors of foods and drinks. But what happens if some of these senses are blocked? Is it harder to tell what you're eating?

You will need: cotton, small jars with lids, stick-on labels, pencil, notebook, juices and drinks (such as apple, orange, tomato, pineapple, grapefruit, cranberry, and milk).

Sniff test

1 Try the sniff test on your friends. Put cotton balls into some small jars. Label each jar. Make a list in your notebook of which juice or drink you will put into each jar. Keep the list secret!

2 Pour onto the cotton ball in each jar the chosen juice or drink. Put the lids on the jars to stop the smells and odors from escaping and mingling together in the air nearby, which could be confusing.

3 Ask your friends to take off the lids and sniff each jar, one by one, without looking inside. The only clue they have is smell. There is no sight, taste, or touch. Can they identify what item is in each jar?

Taste test

Fading tastes

Why do the first few lollipop licks taste best? If you keep eating the same thing, its taste gradually fades. The flavor molecules are still there, but the tongue becomes less sensitive to them. The same happens with smells. It is called habituation.

M A T E R I A L S

You will need: apple, banana, cheese, bread, pear, melon (and similar pale and moist foods), safe knife, blindfold.

1 Try the taste test on your friends. Carefully peel each food and cut it into small cubes to help remove information gained by sight. Try to choose pale-looking foods to remove clues given by colors.

2 Shape can be detected by sight and, also, by the touch sensors in the mouth. To better remove these clues, ask your friend to put on a blindfold.

3 When you have cubed all the foods, ask your friend to chew each one a few times and swallow it. There are hardly any clues from smell or touch. Are the foods easy to identify by taste alone?

NERVES AND BRAIN

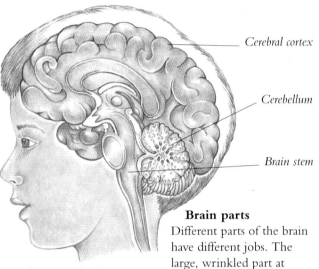

Cerebral cortex

Cerebellum

Brain stem

HAVE you used your brain today? Of course! Perhaps you have thought hard to solve a problem or managed to remember something. Thoughts, memories, ideas, and wishes all happen in the brain. They are in the form of tiny electrical pulses, called nerve signals. These signals whirl around in the brain's complicated network of long, thin nerves – millions of them. Much more happens in the brain, too. It is where you feel emotions like love, fear, and anger. It is where signals are sent from the senses. It is where you decide to make movements and actions. It is also the control center for all your body's inner processes, like heartbeat, breathing, and digesting food. The brain is truly the control center for the entire body.

Brain parts
Different parts of the brain have different jobs. The large, wrinkled part at the top, the cerebral cortex, is where you think, remember, decide, and become aware of what is happening. The cerebellum at the lower rear makes your movements smooth and coordinated. The lowest part, the brain stem, controls basic life processes like heartbeat.

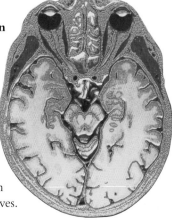

Safe brain
The brain is very delicate, but it is well protected against knocks by the hard skull bone around it. Even so, it is always wise to wear a helmet during physical activities to avoid injury.

Seeing the brain
Medical scanners used in hospitals can see inside the head without any pain or damage – and without cutting it open. Scanners reveal any injury or disease. This false-color picture shows the wrinkled cerebral cortex and the two eyes with their optic nerves.

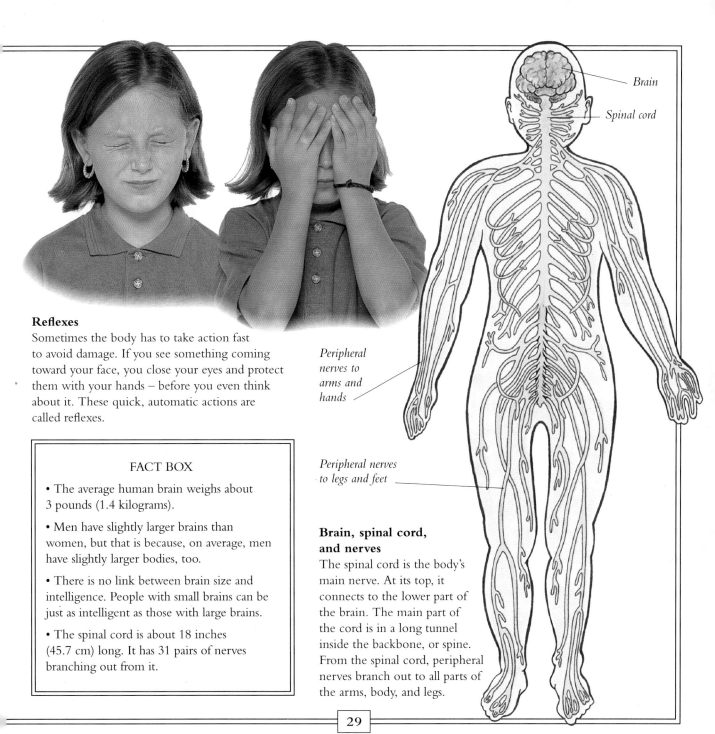

Reflexes

Sometimes the body has to take action fast to avoid damage. If you see something coming toward your face, you close your eyes and protect them with your hands – before you even think about it. These quick, automatic actions are called reflexes.

Brain

Spinal cord

Peripheral nerves to arms and hands

Peripheral nerves to legs and feet

FACT BOX

• The average human brain weighs about 3 pounds (1.4 kilograms).

• Men have slightly larger brains than women, but that is because, on average, men have slightly larger bodies, too.

• There is no link between brain size and intelligence. People with small brains can be just as intelligent as those with large brains.

• The spinal cord is about 18 inches (45.7 cm) long. It has 31 pairs of nerves branching out from it.

Brain, spinal cord, and nerves

The spinal cord is the body's main nerve. At its top, it connects to the lower part of the brain. The main part of the cord is in a long tunnel inside the backbone, or spine. From the spinal cord, peripheral nerves branch out to all parts of the arms, body, and legs.

AWAKE AND ASLEEP

W HEN you wake up in the morning, and it feels as if you have had a good rest, most of your body has. But some parts, like your heart and lungs, have been working all night. Your brain also has been busy doing various activities. No one knows exactly what, or why, but they must be important, because people who cannot sleep become confused and suffer headaches and other pains. They might even collapse.

When the brain and body need sleep, you feel tired. If you ignore this feeling, you may fall asleep anyway. Young children can fall asleep almost anywhere!

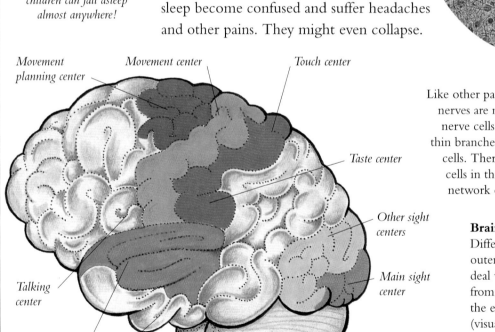

Movement planning center

Movement center

Touch center

Taste center

Other sight centers

Main sight center

Talking center

Hearing center

Smell center (in middle of brain)

Cerebellum for movement coordination

Nerve cells
Like other parts of the body, the brain and nerves are made of cells. They are called nerve cells or neurons. They have long, thin branches that connect to other nerve cells. There are about 100 billion nerve cells in the brain, forming an immense network of pathways for nerve signals.

Brain centers
Different parts of the brain's outer surface, the cerebral cortex, deal with nerve signals coming from the senses. The signals from the eyes arrive at the seeing (visual) center at the back. They are sorted and compared with patterns of signals already in the brain's memory. In this way, you recognize what you see. Other senses have similar centers.

The sides of the brain

The brain looks the same on each side, but the sides have different main activities. The left side takes charge in logic and reasoning, like solving problems in a step-by-step manner, working with numbers, writing, and speaking words. The right side takes the lead in creative and artistic processes, like having ideas, recognizing patterns, painting pictures, and making music.

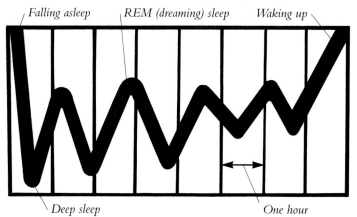

Falling asleep   *REM (dreaming) sleep*   *Waking up*

Deep sleep   *One hour*

Sleep and dreams

When you nod off each night, you first go into deep sleep. Body processes, such as heartbeat and breathing, slow down, and muscles relax. After a time, these processes speed up slightly. Muscles twitch and eyes flicker under closed lids. This is REM (rapid eye movement) sleep, when dreams usually happen. Then, you go into deep sleep again, and so on, through the night.

The night shift

You do not stay completely still all night. Otherwise, you would squash the nerves, blood vessels, and other body parts you are lying on. You move and shift your position as many as 50 times.

FACT BOX

• A newborn baby needs about 20 hours of sleep each day.

• A 10-year-old needs about 10 hours of sleep each night.

• An adult needs 7-8 hours of sleep each night.

• These numbers are averages. Some people need less sleep, and others need more.

MEMORIES

M A T E R I A L S

Some people write about their lives in a diary. This is a memory aid. They can look up a day that happened long ago. From a few words in the diary, they can begin to recall many other things that happened. The few words act as a memory trigger.

THERE is not one place in the brain for memories. They seem to be spread through several brain parts. Memories are probably complicated connections and pathways for nerve signals among the brain's millions of nerve cells. There are two stages to making a memory. One is to remember, which is to store the information in your brain. The other is to recall it, which is to find it again. You can play a sport or musical instrument better with practice. It is the same with memories. The more practice you have trying to remember, the better you should become. There are also a few memory aids, short-cuts, and "tricks" that you can use, *as shown*.

You will need for the memory tray: a selection of household toys, ornaments, utensils, and similar small items.

Memory test

1 Lay out on a table a row of about eight or ten small, everyday objects. Have a friend look at them for about 20 seconds, then try to remember their names and their positions in the row.

2 Have your friend close her/his eyes while you move two objects to switch their positions. Can your friend identify the moved items? This is usually easier than remembering all the items in order.

3 Study all the objects again and try to memorize them. One trick is to make a word from the first letter of each of their names. Or try to include their names in a silly story, which makes them easier to recall.

Memories in smells and pictures

A smell or a picture triggers your memory by taking your mind back to where and when you smelled the smell or saw what is in the picture.

Picture memory game

Luck and judgment

Some games are partly luck, but you usually can play them better if you train yourself to remember certain things. You can figure out where a card is in the deck by remembering the cards before it.

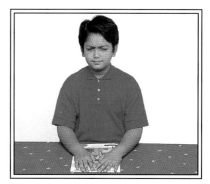

1 Some people find that they can remember pictures better than numbers and words. Try this picture memory test. Look at pictures in a book for 20 seconds. Note their shapes, colors, and other details.

2 Now, concentrate on the picture memories in your mind. Keep going through each part, so it stays "fresh." Repeat the details of the shapes, shading, and colors and repeat the names of any objects.

3 After another 20 seconds, close the book and describe the pictures or draw them. Get friends to try the same test. Do it several times. With practice, you gradually should become more skilled.

FOOD FOR THE BODY

IF you do not eat a meal for many hours, you soon begin to feel hungry. This is your body's way of telling you that it needs more energy to power its thousands of chemical life processes. It needs more nutrients (raw materials), too, for repairs, growth, and body maintenance. So you eat. Food contains both energy and nutrients. Some animals eat only one kind of food. Pandas feed on bamboo, and koalas munch only on eucalyptus leaves. But the human body needs a wide variety of foods to stay healthy. In particular, fresh vegetables and fruits are very good for the human body.

Imagine what you eat in a typical month. It probably adds up to about 100 pounds (45 kg) of food, plus 50 quarts (liters) of drinks. Even more amazing, it turns into you!

Carbohydrates and fiber
Carbohydrates are the body's main energy source. They are found in rice, potatoes, bread, and pasta. Fiber (roughage) is not fully digested, but it gives food bulk and texture, and it keeps the intestines working. Whole grains (like oats), vegetables, and fruits have plenty of fiber.

Proteins and fats
Proteins provide raw materials for maintenance and growth. Proteins are found in meat, fish, dairy products, and some vegetables, such as peas and beans. Fats are needed in fairly small amounts for healthy nerves and other parts of the body.

34

Food gives you energy

The energy in food is measured in calories. A slice of whole-grain bread contains about 60 calories, plus useful vitamins, minerals, and fiber. A bar of chocolate contains 250 calories but little else. Your energy needs depend mainly on how active you are. If you eat too much high-energy food and don't work it off, the body converts the extra calories to fat.

Resting uses about 1 calorie per minute.

Walking or gentle activity uses 3 calories per minute.

Running or hard exercise uses 7 calories per minute.

Fruits

Most fruits, such as passion fruit and strawberries, are good sources of sugar for energy, as well as vitamins, minerals, and fiber.

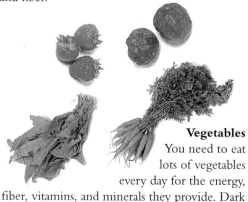

Vegetables

You need to eat lots of vegetables every day for the energy, fiber, vitamins, and minerals they provide. Dark green vegetables are especially good for you.

The body contains an amazing assortment of minerals and substances, including iron (as in nails) and sulfur (as in matches) – and the body is three-fifths water!

MOUTH AND TEETH

THE first stop for the body's food is the mouth, with its various parts: teeth, lips, cheeks, and tongue. Each part has a job to do. The teeth bite off pieces of food and chew and squash and mash them. The lips open to let the food in, then seal together so that it does not fall out. The cheeks bulge as the tongue moves the food around between the teeth for thorough chewing. As food is chewed, it is mixed with watery saliva to make it soft and moist. Then, the tongue pushes the mashed lump of food back into the throat for swallowing down into the stomach. All the mouth's chewing work helps digest food.

If an item of food is too big for your mouth, you can try to break it with your fingers or cut it up with a knife. But the easiest way usually is to bite off a piece using your sharp front teeth, the incisors.

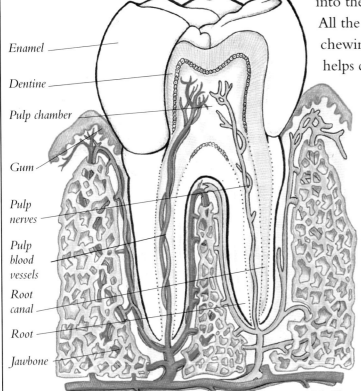

Enamel

Dentine

Pulp chamber

Gum

Pulp nerves

Pulp blood vessels

Root canal

Root

Jawbone

Inside a tooth

A tooth's upper part, the crown, is covered with whitish enamel, the hardest substance in the body. Underneath is dentine, which is slightly softer to absorb knocks and great pressure. The tooth's lower part, the root, anchors it in the jawbone. At the center is a living pulp of blood vessels that provide nourishment and nerves that warn of too much pressure or dental decay – toothache! Brush your teeth morning and night, after every meal, if possible, to remove leftover food and germs that cause tooth decay. Visit the dentist regularly for a check-up and advice on cleaning and flossing.

Enamel

This cross-section of a tooth *(above)*, magnified 275 times, shows that tooth enamel forms from thousands of tiny rods.

Diets of the past

We can tell what people have eaten, even after they die, from the shapes of their teeth and the tiny marks and scratches on tooth surfaces. These clues show that prehistoric people, such as Heidelberg Man, who lived, perhaps, a half million years ago, ate plenty of tough plant roots and shoots.

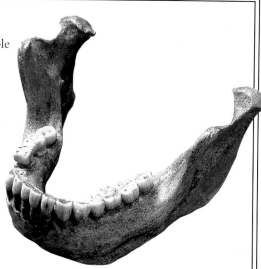

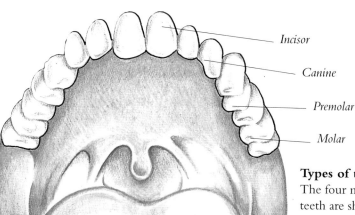

Incisor

Canine

Premolar

Molar

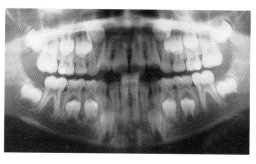

Types of teeth

The four main kinds of teeth are shaped to do different jobs. Incisors, at the front, are wide and sharp-edged, like chisels, for biting and nibbling. Canines are longer and more pointed to tear and rip. Premolars and molars, at the back, are broad and fairly flat to squash and crush.

Hidden teeth

A dental x-ray shows a child's adult teeth under the milk teeth. From about the age of six, the milk teeth fall out and are replaced by the adult or permanent teeth. In each half of each jaw (upper and lower), a child has two incisors, one canine, and two molars, making a total of 20 teeth. An adult has two incisors, one canine, two premolars, and three molars, making a total of 32 teeth.

THE DIGESTIVE SYSTEM

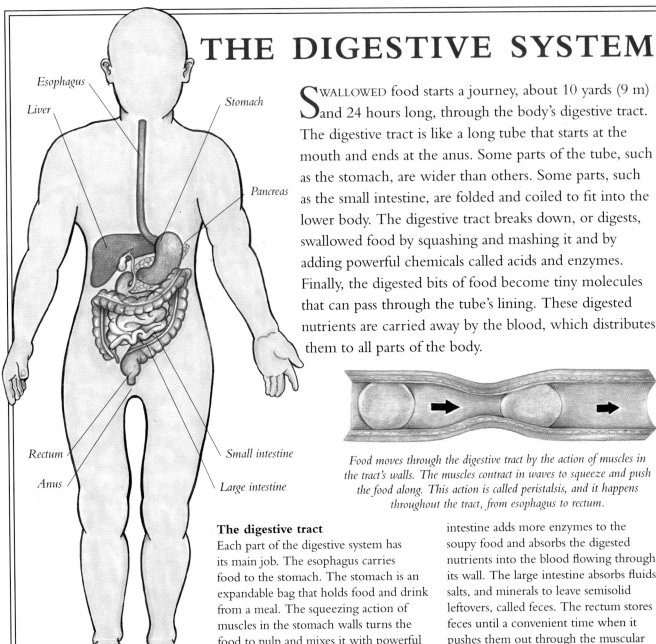

Esophagus

Liver

Stomach

Pancreas

Rectum

Anus

Small intestine

Large intestine

Swallowed food starts a journey, about 10 yards (9 m) and 24 hours long, through the body's digestive tract. The digestive tract is like a long tube that starts at the mouth and ends at the anus. Some parts of the tube, such as the stomach, are wider than others. Some parts, such as the small intestine, are folded and coiled to fit into the lower body. The digestive tract breaks down, or digests, swallowed food by squashing and mashing it and by adding powerful chemicals called acids and enzymes. Finally, the digested bits of food become tiny molecules that can pass through the tube's lining. These digested nutrients are carried away by the blood, which distributes them to all parts of the body.

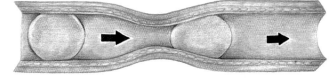

Food moves through the digestive tract by the action of muscles in the tract's walls. The muscles contract in waves to squeeze and push the food along. This action is called peristalsis, and it happens throughout the tract, from esophagus to rectum.

The digestive tract
Each part of the digestive system has its main job. The esophagus carries food to the stomach. The stomach is an expandable bag that holds food and drink from a meal. The squeezing action of muscles in the stomach walls turns the food to pulp and mixes it with powerful digestive acids and enzymes. The small intestine adds more enzymes to the soupy food and absorbs the digested nutrients into the blood flowing through its wall. The large intestine absorbs fluids, salts, and minerals to leave semisolid leftovers, called feces. The rectum stores feces until a convenient time when it pushes them out through the muscular ring of the anus.

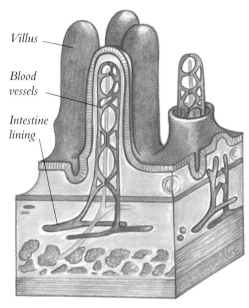

Villus

Blood vessels

Intestine lining

Digestion times
The amount of time it takes food to travel through your digestive system depends on how easy that food is to digest.

Mouth
(minutes for each swallow)

Esophagus
(seconds for each swallow)

Stomach
(1 to 6 hours)

Small intestine
(2 to 15 hours)

Large intestine
(6 to 24 hours)

Anus
(12 to 24 hours)

Inside the intestine
The small intestine lining has thousands of tiny, short hairlike parts called villi, which provide a large surface area for absorbing food. Each villus has blood vessels that carry the digested food to where it is needed.

Digestive juices
Tiny pits in the lining of the stomach (*above*) and between the villi of the small intestine ooze digestive juices. These juices consist of enzymes and powerful acids that break down the food.

FACT BOX

• The esophagus is about 10 inches (25 cm) long and 1 inch (2.5 cm) wide.

• The stomach can expand to hold more than 1 1/2 quarts (liters) of foods and fluids.

• The small intestine is 20 feet (6 m) long and 1 inch (2.5 cm) wide.

• The large intestine, or colon, is 5 feet (1.5 m) long and 2 inches (5 cm) wide.

• The rectum is 6 inches (15 cm) long and 2 inches (5 cm) wide.

Parts of the system
The liver and pancreas are not part of the digestive tract, but they are part of the digestive system. The liver receives blood, loaded with nutrients, from the small intestine. It processes, stores, changes, and distributes the nutrients according to the body's needs. The pancreas makes digestive enzymes that pour into the small intestine to help break down food.

EATING AND DRINKING

OOD provides fuel for the body. A delicious meal also gives us great enjoyment and pleasure. For some people, cooking food is a skill or an interesting pastime – or even an obsession! Food also gives us the opportunity to take a break and meet others. When we sit down for a meal, we have time to pause from the rush of the day, think, and consider what to do next. We can appreciate the meal and drinks and chat and talk with family and friends. Trying to eat while moving around or doing other things can cause problems. We may not chew thoroughly, and unchewed food could choke us.

Many important events include food, from the ice cream and cake of a birthday party to the many courses of a banquet at a wedding.

M A T E R I A L S

You will need: crackers or dry cookies, a beverage.

Make your mouth water

A moist mouth

Watery saliva is made in three pairs of salivary glands around the face. Saliva moistens and softens food as you chew, so that you can mash it into a squishy pulp and swallow it easily. Saliva also begins the chemical breakdown, or digestion, of the starch in food. Normally, we do not notice saliva and what it does because many foods are moist. But, if you eat very dry foods, you soon notice its absence.

1 Bite off a piece of cracker or cookie. Chew slowly. Can you feel your saliva making this dry food damp and soft? Swallow, then eat another piece.

2 Eat some more. Salivary glands make about 1 quart (liter) of saliva daily, but only a limited amount in a few minutes, less than 4 ounces (120 milliliters).

3 How many crackers or cookies can you eat before they become too dry and hard to chew? Your saliva is used up. You need a drink to finish the job.

Strange-looking foods

Before we eat, we check that a meal is safe to eat. We sniff for its smell, and we look at it to identify the foods. Are they the right shape and color? If foods appear odd, such as different colors than normal, we might be worried about eating them. This is a natural reaction or instinct. Blue foods, such as this blue pasta, look especially odd. Can you think of more than two or three natural, safe blue foods?

Funny texture

The appearance of food in terms of texture is important, too. Fish sticks, fried eggs, and vegetables normally look tasty, but, if you mash them up, you probably wouldn't want them anymore!

MATERIALS

You will need: bread, scales, supervised use of an oven.

The body needs about 3 quarts (liters) of water every day. Some of this is in the form of food, the rest as drinks. How much water is in food?

Water in food

1 Carefully weigh a slice of bread. Ask an adult to put the bread in a suitable container in the oven. Heat the bread until it is dry, but not burned.

2 Let the bread cool. Weigh it again. What proportion was water, now evaporated? Repeat these steps with other types of food.

BODY WASTES

ALL animals produce waste, from small mouse droppings to huge mounds of elephant dung. The human body does, too. Like cats, dogs, and similar creatures, it makes two main kinds of wastes. There are solid wastes (also called feces or bowel movements) and liquid wastes (urine). These two kinds of wastes have very different origins. Feces are the leftovers at the end of the digestive process. They come out of the end of the digestive tract, the anus. Urine is mainly chemical waste and excess water filtered from the blood by body parts called the kidneys. It comes from the bladder. The body also produces a waste gas called carbon dioxide, which is breathed out through the lungs.

You will need: large and small plastic funnels, tape.

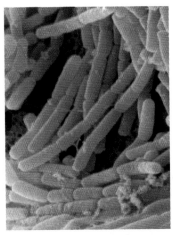

Not all microbes are harmful germs. These friendly bacteria live in everyone's intestines, and they help with digestion.

Listen to your tummy

1 You can hear wastes gurgling through your intestines. Push together the spouts of a large and a small funnel, *as shown.*

2 Tape the spouts together. The large funnel acts as a sound collector for body noises such as digestion or heartbeat.

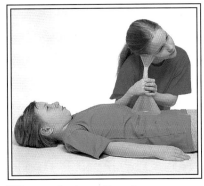

3 Press the large funnel onto a friend's abdomen and the small one around your ear. Can you hear food slurping and gases bubbling?

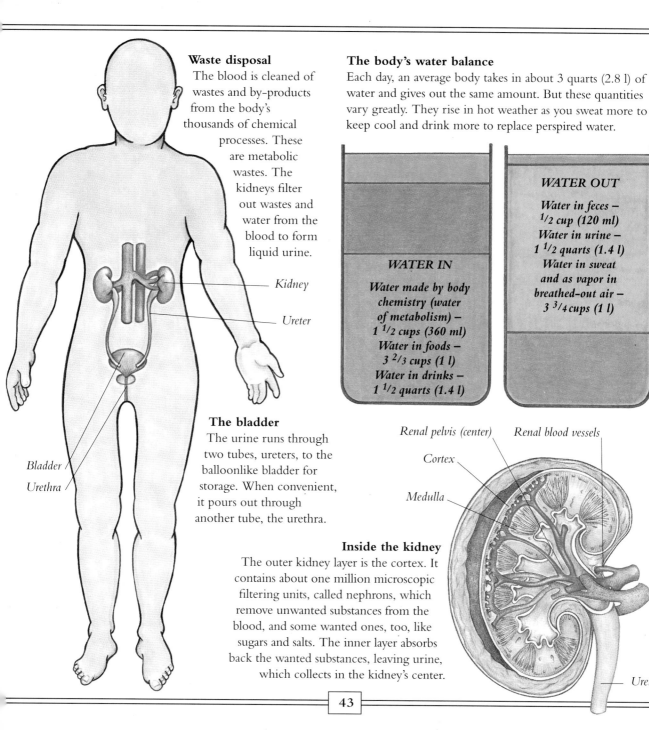

Waste disposal

The blood is cleaned of wastes and by-products from the body's thousands of chemical processes. These are metabolic wastes. The kidneys filter out wastes and water from the blood to form liquid urine.

Kidney

Ureter

The body's water balance

Each day, an average body takes in about 3 quarts (2.8 l) of water and gives out the same amount. But these quantities vary greatly. They rise in hot weather as you sweat more to keep cool and drink more to replace perspired water.

WATER IN

Water made by body chemistry (water of metabolism) –
1 1/2 cups (360 ml)
Water in foods –
3 2/3 cups (1 l)
Water in drinks –
1 1/2 quarts (1.4 l)

WATER OUT

Water in feces –
1/2 cup (120 ml)
Water in urine –
1 1/2 quarts (1.4 l)
Water in sweat and as vapor in breathed-out air –
3 3/4 cups (1 l)

The bladder

The urine runs through two tubes, ureters, to the balloonlike bladder for storage. When convenient, it pours out through another tube, the urethra.

Bladder
Urethra

Renal pelvis (center)   *Renal blood vessels*

Cortex

Medulla

Inside the kidney

The outer kidney layer is the cortex. It contains about one million microscopic filtering units, called nephrons, which remove unwanted substances from the blood, and some wanted ones, too, like sugars and salts. The inner layer absorbs back the wanted substances, leaving urine, which collects in the kidney's center.

Ureter

LUNGS AND BREATHING

ALL animals need oxygen to live. Oxygen is an invisible gas in the air around us. It is required for part of the chemical changes that happen in every body cell, to break down digested foods and nutrients, and to get energy from them. This energy powers muscles and the body's life processes. The series of chemical changes is called aerobic respiration. The body cannot store oxygen, so it must get fresh supplies every minute. It does this by breathing (respiring). The body parts involved in breathing and absorbing oxygen from the air are called the respiratory system. They include the nose, throat, and windpipe (trachea), and the two spongy, cone-shaped lungs in the chest.

Your two lungs normally hold about 13 cubic feet (0.36 cubic meters) of air. But, when your body is very active and you breathe in very deeply, they hold over 25 cubic feet (0.7 cubic meters) of air.

People can hold their breath for a minute or so when swimming underwater. For longer periods, however, we need to take along an oxygen supply. Oxygen is contained as pressurized air inside scuba tanks.

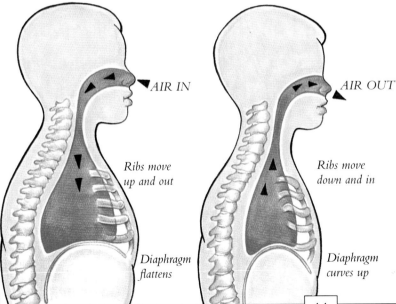

AIR IN

Ribs move up and out

Diaphragm flattens

AIR OUT

Ribs move down and in

Diaphragm curves up

Muscles for breathing

The movements of breathing are called bodily respiration. They are made by two main sets of muscles. One is the diaphragm, a sheet of muscle under the lungs. The other set is the intercostals, short muscles between each pair of ribs.

In and out

To breathe in, the diaphragm contracts to become shorter and flatter, and the lungs stretch downward. The intercostals contract, pulling up the ribs, which stretches the lungs forward. The stretched lungs draw in air. To breathe out, the diaphragm and intercostals relax. The stretched lungs spring back and blow out air.

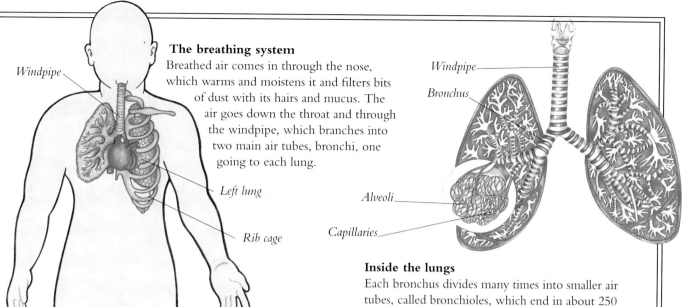

The breathing system

Breathed air comes in through the nose, which warms and moistens it and filters bits of dust with its hairs and mucus. The air goes down the throat and through the windpipe, which branches into two main air tubes, bronchi, one going to each lung.

Windpipe

Left lung

Rib cage

Windpipe

Bronchus

Alveoli

Capillaries

Inside the lungs

Each bronchus divides many times into smaller air tubes, called bronchioles, which end in about 250 million microscopic air bubbles, called alveoli. The alveoli are surrounded by networks of microscopic blood vessels, called capillaries. Oxygen from the alveoli seeps into the blood in the capillaries to be pumped around the body.

Fair exchange

Breathing not only takes oxygen into the body, it also gets rid of carbon dioxide, a waste product made in cells by aerobic respiration. Carbon dioxide is collected by the blood and passes into the air in the lungs, to be breathed out. If carbon dioxide built up in the blood, it soon would poison the body.

FACT BOX

• At rest, an average person breathes in and out about 14 to 16 times per minute.

• After lots of exercise, this resting rate can rise to more than 60 times per minute.

• At rest, an average person breathes in and out 30 cubic inches (492 cubic centimeters) of air.

• After exercise, this volume of air can rise to more than 10 cubic feet (0.3 cubic meters).

• At rest, new babies breathe in and out much faster than adults, 40 to 50 times per minute. By age five, this rate slows to 25 times per minute.

BREATHED-IN AIR	BREATHED-OUT AIR
Nitrogen – 78 percent	Nitrogen – 79 percent
Oxygen – 21 percent	Oxygen – 16 percent
Carbon dioxide – 0.04 percent	Carbon dioxide – 4 percent
Plus other gases	Plus other gases

BREATHING AND BLOWING

Breathing has many uses, in addition to obtaining oxygen. As air passes through the voice box, or larynx, in your neck, it allows you to talk and sing. If you purse your lips, or blow through a narrow gap between your fingers, you can whistle. If you blow out hard, you can spin pinwheels and inflate balloons. When you blow out forcefully like this, you use extra muscles in your abdomen and chest. Breathing also operates many musical instruments, from recorders to trumpets and tubas.

Hold pinwheels in front of your mouth and breathe normally. Do they spin? Blow gently, then hard. Do they move? Try different breathing-type actions, such as talking, shouting, and whistling. Which spins the pinwheels fastest?

Don't blow too hard

As you blow up a balloon, you force air from your lungs up through your windpipe and mouth into the balloon. This requires lots of muscle power in your chest and abdomen and great air pressure in your lungs. If you try too hard for too long, it could damage the lungs' delicate air bubbles (alveoli) that take in oxygen. An air pump for blowing up balloons is much less risky!

How fast do you breathe?

Use a stopwatch or similar timepiece to time your breaths. Breathing in, then out, is one breath. Count the number of breaths in 30 seconds, then double it to find the rate per minute. Do various activities to see how they affect your rate of breathing. Rest for 5 minutes and count your breaths. How do you compare with the average rates on the previous page? Next, say your favorite nursery rhyme several times. Count your breaths as you do this. (Talking as you breathe out is the out-breath.) Then, run in place for 5 minutes and count the rate again. How fast does it get?

46

You will need: water, large shallow bowl, large glass or clear plastic jar or jug, a length of tubing.

The breath machine

You can compare the amounts of air you breathe when doing different activities by using this homemade version of the scientific device called a spirometer. You breathe out air through the tube, and it bubbles into the water-filled jar and pushes the water out. The lower the water level in the jar after the breath, the bigger the volume of that breath.

4 Take a breath. Then carefully breathe out into the tube.

The water level in the jar shows the volume of breathed-out air.

WARNING

Never breathe in through the tube, or you could cough and choke on water!

How much air?

1 Half-fill the large shallow bowl with water and put it on a firm surface. Also, completely fill the large jar with water.

2 Put the tubing into the large bowl. With your hand sealed over the jar's mouth, quickly turn it upside down.

3 Put the jar in the bowl and take your hand away. The water should stay in the jar. Put one end of the tube into the jar under the rim.

TALKING

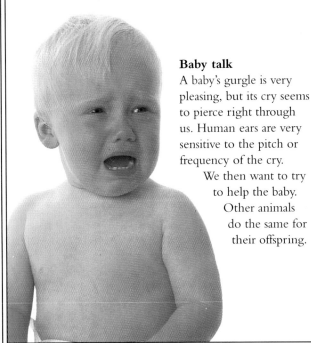

Birds, such as parrots and mynahs, can imitate many sounds, from the noise of a car or telephone to words of human speech. But the bird does not understand or mean what it says.

TALKING is a natural, everyday part of life. Humans are generally social creatures and like to be in groups with family and friends. Speech is our main form of communication. We talk about books, movies, television programs, sports, wishes and wants, and how we think and feel. The sounds of speech are made possible by the vocal cords in the larynx (voice box), which is in the neck. Along with the lungs and the windpipe, the larynx is part of the respiratory system. We also communicate by making facial expressions (like smiles and frowns), by using our hands, and by our general body posture, behavior, and movements. These expressions and gestures are called body language. In the right situation, a small yet silent movement of part of the body can say more than words ever could.

Baby talk
A baby's gurgle is very pleasing, but its cry seems to pierce right through us. Human ears are very sensitive to the pitch or frequency of the cry. We then want to try to help the baby. Other animals do the same for their offspring.

Meaning without talking
The vocal cords make many sounds besides speech. We laugh, cry, sob, and hum. These sounds and many others are called vocalizations. They convey messages, such as happiness or sadness. The loudness and other features of a sound also are important. A loud, short shout usually means a warning. Whispering "sweet nothings" shows affection.

Shaping the sounds

Vibrations from the vocal cords themselves are surprisingly quiet and indistinct. We make them into clear words and other vocal sounds using the mouth, lips, teeth, tongue, and cheeks. Look in a mirror and see how these parts move as you make different sounds, such as *f, m, o, e, and l.*

Vocal cord

Gap between cords

During speech, the gap almost closes.

Louder and louder

In some places, like a crowded concert hall, the human voice is not loud enough. We use electrical power to make it louder. A microphone works like a human ear, changing the voice's sound waves into tiny pulses of electricity. An amplifier makes the sound much stronger. The pulses feed into a loudspeaker, which works like the vocal cords, vibrating to reproduce the sound waves, but much more loudly.

Inside the voice box

Vocal sounds come from the larynx at the top of the windpipe. It has two flaps, called vocal cords, attached to its sides. The gap between them, called the glottis, is for normal breathing. To speak, laryngeal muscles pull the vocal cords together, so there is hardly any gap. Air flows past, making them vibrate to produce sounds. The tighter they close, the higher the sound.

BLOOD AND ITS TUBES

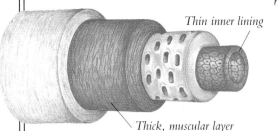

Thin inner lining

Thick, muscular layer

Arteries

These blood vessels carry blood away from the heart. They have thick, elastic walls to withstand the high pressure of blood as it surges from the heart with each beat. They divide many times, becoming smaller until they form capillaries.

To stay alive, all the cells in the body need continuing supplies of oxygen, energy, and nutrients. And they all produce waste substances that must be removed. The blood is the body's transport system – its delivery and collection service. Blood delivers oxygen (from the lungs) and raw materials, such as energy-rich sugars and other nutrients (from digestion), for use by cells. It collects carbon dioxide for removal by the lungs and wastes to be filtered by the kidneys. Blood can do all this because it flows around every part and in every corner of the body in a vast network of branching tubes, called blood vessels. It flows because it is pumped by regular contractions of a hollow bag of muscle – the heart. The heart, blood vessels, and blood are called the circulatory system.

Wall one cell thick

Capillaries

Capillaries are barely 0.04 inch (1 mm) long and far too thin to see. Oxygen, nutrients, and other substances seep through their walls to the cells beyond. Capillaries join to make veins.

Veins

Veins carry blood back to the heart. They are thin-walled and floppy, since blood has lost most of its surging pressure after passing through the microscopic capillaries.

Thin outer wall

Thin inner lining

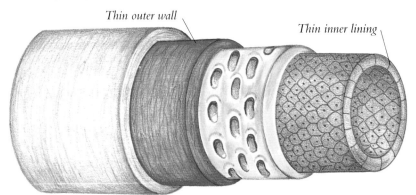

The blood system

The network of arteries, capillaries, and veins spreads through the entire body, even into bones and muscles. The large blood vessels have individual names and are in much the same place in each human body. The smaller ones vary from one person to another.

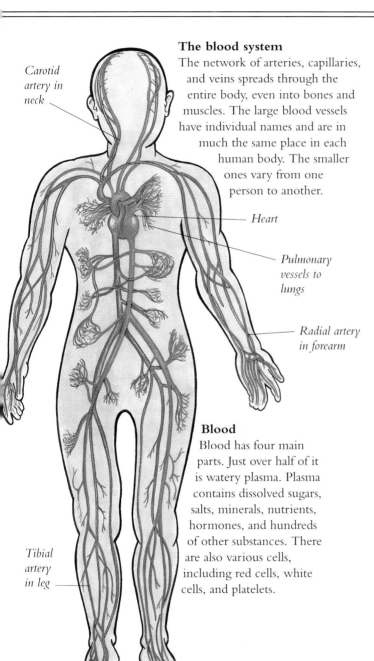

Carotid artery in neck

Heart

Pulmonary vessels to lungs

Radial artery in forearm

Tibial artery in leg

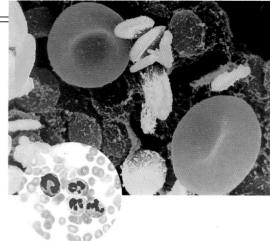

Blood cells

Blood contains millions of cells. Red blood cells (colored red in the picture *above*) carry oxygen. They pick it up in the capillaries in the lungs and take it to the cells all around the body. Platelets (colored yellow in the picture *above*) help blood clot to seal a cut or a wound. White blood cells *(in the circle)* clean the blood and body tissues and fight germs. They can surround and "eat" germs, dead cells, and other debris.

Blood

Blood has four main parts. Just over half of it is watery plasma. Plasma contains dissolved sugars, salts, minerals, nutrients, hormones, and hundreds of other substances. There are also various cells, including red cells, white cells, and platelets.

FACT BOX

• An average adult body has about 5 quarts (4.7 l) of blood.

• At any moment, three-quarters of the blood is in the veins, one-fifth is in the arteries, and the remaining one-twentieth is in the capillaries.

• If all the blood vessels in the body were joined end to end, they would stretch 62,000 miles (99,758 kilometers), which is two and a half times around the earth.

HEART AND HEARTBEAT

THE beating heart is the symbol of life. If the heart stops pumping, blood stops flowing. The blood can no longer deliver nutrients, especially oxygen, to the body. Without oxygen, and with wastes building up, cells begin to die within minutes. The heart is like a hollow bag with very strong, muscular walls. As the muscles contract, they squeeze blood from inside the heart into the arteries. As the muscles relax, more blood flows into the heart from the veins. The heart's thick walls are made from a special type of muscle, called cardiac muscle.

...lub-dub, lub-dub...

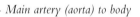

Main artery (aorta) to body

Pulmonary arteries to lungs

Pulmonary veins from lungs

Left atrium

Right atrium

One-way valve

Left ventricle

Right ventricle

Muscular wall of heart

The heart is between the lungs in the middle of the chest, slightly to the left side, protected by the breastbone and ribs. It is about the size of its owner's clenched fist.

Inside the heart

The heart is not one pump, but two. Each pump has a small upper chamber, the atrium, and a large lower one, the ventricle. One-way valves inside the heart make blood flow the appropriate way (from the atrium to the ventricle and into the arteries), rather than just sloshing back and forth with each heartbeat.

The stages of a heartbeat

The heartbeat is one smooth and continuous process, but it can be shown in stages to see what happens.

1. Blood flows from the main veins into the small upper chambers on each side, the atria.

2. The atria squeeze blood through one-way valves into the lower chambers, the ventricles, which have much thicker muscle walls.

3. The ventricles fill with blood, and their muscular walls begin to contract powerfully.

4. Blood is forced at high pressure, through more one-way valves, from the ventricles out into the main arteries.

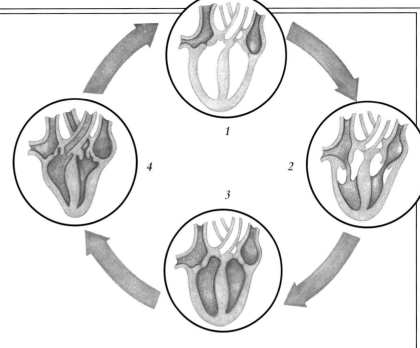

1

2

3

4

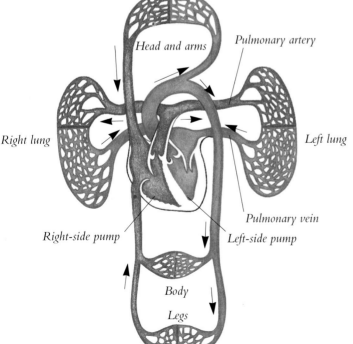

Head and arms

Pulmonary artery

Right lung

Left lung

Pulmonary vein

Right-side pump

Left-side pump

Body

Legs

Blood around the body

Blood flows around the body in two stages. It leaves the heart's left side and goes into the branching arteries, capillaries, and veins of the main body, head, arms, and legs. This is systemic circulation, delivering oxygen and nutrients to body cells.

Blood to the lungs

After going around the body, low-oxygen blood goes into the heart's right side. It then is pumped to the lungs, in the pulmonary arteries, to pick up more oxygen and become bright red. This is pulmonary circulation. Blood then goes back to the heart's left side to be pumped on to the body, and the journey goes on in a never-ending, continuous flow. An average trip around the systemic and pulmonary circulations takes one minute.

PULSE

EACH time the heart beats, it sends a surge of pressurized blood into the body's arteries. The pressure makes the elastic artery walls bulge outward. This bulging happens in all the arteries spreading out from the heart. The pulsations or bulges are easiest to feel in arteries that are near the surface of the body, just under the skin. They are called the pulse, and there is one pulsation for each heartbeat. So counting the pulse rate is the same as counting the heartbeat rate. When the body is active or excited, the pulse rate goes up – the heart is beating faster to send more energy and oxygen in the blood to the muscles, so that they can be active. Heart rate is under the control of nerve signals from the brain. It also is affected by adrenaline – one of the chemicals, called hormones, which control many body processes.

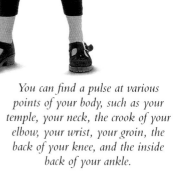

You can find a pulse at various points of your body, such as your temple, your neck, the crook of your elbow, your wrist, your groin, the back of your knee, and the inside back of your ankle.

Finding the pulse
Put two fingers on the inside of the wrist, just below the base of the lower thumb. Do not use your thumb because it has a fairly strong pulse of its own. Press gently and feel for the pulsating artery in the hollow next to the hard, cordlike tendons in the wrist. Count the number of pulses in one minute.

How the pulse rate varies

Changes in pulse rate with exercise can indicate the body's general fitness. Measure your pulse rate at rest, every minute after walking 5 minutes, and every minute after running 2 minutes. The time taken for the rate to return to normal is called the recovery time. Usually, the shorter it is, the better.

You will need: scissors, adhesive, drinking straw, stopwatch or clock.

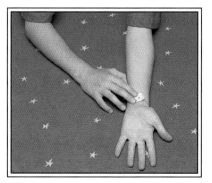

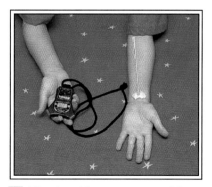

See your pulse

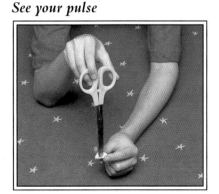

1 You can "see" a pulse, rather than feel it, with this pulse-meter. With scissors, carefully make a hole in a small piece of adhesive.

2 Feel for the wrist pulse. Press the adhesive on that spot, firmly, without flattening it. Push the straw into the hole.

3 The tiny skin movements of the pulse are magnified by the straw. Use a stopwatch to time the pulse as the straw moves back and forth.

BONES AND JOINTS

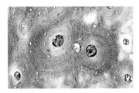

This microscope view inside a bone shows that the bone is made of hundreds of tiny rods packed together. At the center of each rod are miniature blood vessels.

Most parts of the human body are soft and floppy. Nerves, veins, and intestines could not stand up by themselves. So the body has an inner framework, called the skeleton, to give it shape and support. The skeleton is made up of 206 bones. Bones are not white, brittle, flaky, and dead, like you see in museums. Inside a living body, bones are pale gray, strong, tough, and very much alive. Bones are stiff but slightly flexible and usually able to bend under strain, instead of snapping. Like other body parts, bones are made by cells and contain cells. They have their own nerves, blood vessels, and other supplies. They are linked together at joints, so they can move when pulled by muscles.

Knee and elbow joints work like ordinary hinges, while the spine is like a string of beads with the spinal column running down the middle.

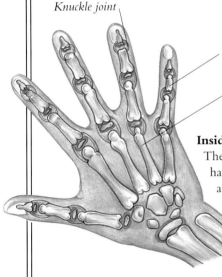

Knuckle joint

Bone in finger

Bone in palm

Inside the hand
The skeleton of the hand has many small bones linked at delicate joints. There are 8 bones in the wrist, 4 in each finger, and 3 in the thumb.

The skull
The dome of the skull is formed by 8 large curved bones fixed together firmly at wiggly joint lines called sutures. Another 13 small bones, also joined at sutures, make up the framework of the face.

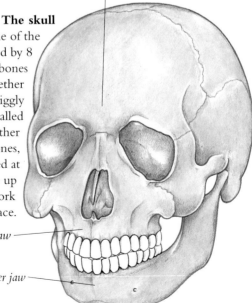

Frontal bone forms the forehead

Upper jaw

Lower jaw

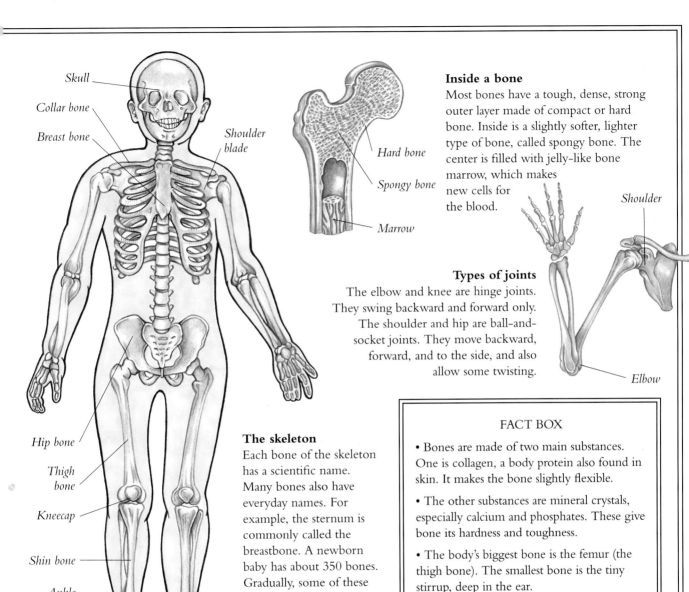

Skull

Collar bone

Breast bone

Shoulder blade

Inside a bone

Most bones have a tough, dense, strong outer layer made of compact or hard bone. Inside is a slightly softer, lighter type of bone, called spongy bone. The center is filled with jelly-like bone marrow, which makes new cells for the blood.

Hard bone

Spongy bone

Marrow

Shoulder

Types of joints

The elbow and knee are hinge joints. They swing backward and forward only. The shoulder and hip are ball-and-socket joints. They move backward, forward, and to the side, and also allow some twisting.

Elbow

Hip bone

Thigh bone

Kneecap

Shin bone

Ankle bones

The skeleton

Each bone of the skeleton has a scientific name. Many bones also have everyday names. For example, the sternum is commonly called the breastbone. A newborn baby has about 350 bones. Gradually, some of these join together during growth. So the average adult has 206 bones.

FACT BOX

• Bones are made of two main substances. One is collagen, a body protein also found in skin. It makes the bone slightly flexible.

• The other substances are mineral crystals, especially calcium and phosphates. These give bone its hardness and toughness.

• The body's biggest bone is the femur (the thigh bone). The smallest bone is the tiny stirrup, deep in the ear.

• Where bones meet in a joint, they are covered with cartilage. Cartilage is shiny and slippery for smooth movements and to prevent the bone ends from wearing away.

MUSCLES

BONES give the body a strong inner framework, and the joints between them allow the bones to bend and straighten. But, without the skeletal muscles to pull the bones, the body could not move. Without the cardiac muscles in the walls of the heart, the blood would not go around the body. Without the muscles in the walls of the esophagus, stomach, and intestines, the body could not push food through its digestive system. Muscles make every movement of the body happen, including inner processes, such as digestion and circulation, and body actions, such as walking and running.

Hundreds of muscles work together as teams to make the body do amazing and skillful actions, from playing tennis to playing a musical instrument.

About 40 facial muscles make expressions of all kinds, especially a wide smile!

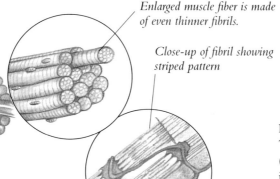

Bundles of muscle fibers

Enlarged muscle fiber is made of even thinner fibrils.

Close-up of fibril showing striped pattern

Muscle

Smooth muscle does not have a striped pattern.

Inside muscle

The three main types of muscles are skeletal (striped or voluntary), visceral (smooth or involuntary), and cardiac (heart). They are all made from groups of large cells which are specialized to contract (get shorter). Skeletal muscles are bundles of huge cells called muscle fibers, almost as thick as hairs. Their movements are voluntary (under the conscious control of your brain).

Pectoral muscle or "pec"

Muscles galore

The body has hundreds of skeletal muscles. They are arranged in layers, and their ends are joined to the bones of the skeleton. This is the outer muscle layer, just under the skin. Beneath is the middle muscle layer, and then an inner layer. Every muscle has a scientific name, but a few of them have common, everyday names.

The smallest muscles are grouped in the hand.

Bigger muscles tend to move bigger parts of the body.

Opposed muscles

Muscles are arranged in opposing pairs or groups. One muscle pulls the bone one way, and the opposing muscle pulls it back again. Although muscles can contract to pull bones, they cannot forcefully lengthen to push them. The end of a muscle tapers into a thin, ropelike tendon joined firmly to a bone.

A muscle at the front of the leg contracts to bend the ankle and toes.

A muscle at the back contracts to straighten the ankle to stand on tiptoe.

MOVING

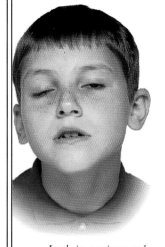

Look in a mirror and exercise your face muscles. You use them to smile, frown, and make other expressions. Contract or stretch each one in turn, in new and unusual ways, to make some very funny faces!

THE muscles, bones, and joints all work together to make the body move. Muscles are controlled by the brain. The brain sends out thousands of nerve signals every second, along the nerves to every muscle, telling muscles when to contract, or pull, and when to relax and stop pulling. Even simple actions like sitting or standing involve dozens of muscles contracting or relaxing at exactly the correct time, by the correct amount, to keep the body's posture upright, well-positioned, and well-balanced. As you grow up, you learn to control your muscles for everyday movements such as standing, walking, talking, running, biting, and chewing. Sometimes, when you are not concentrating, these actions go slightly wrong. You might bite your tongue! When you learn a new action, you have to concentrate hard to coordinate the new movement pattern. Practice makes perfect – well, usually.

Funny fingers

Try moving your fingers apart and then together in two pairs while keeping them straight, *as shown*. Is it easy? If not, can you soon learn to do it smoothly? What about the other hand? Because this hand position is odd and seldom used, it is not very easy to do unless you practice.

Rub and pat

Can you pat your head while rubbing your stomach? How about patting your stomach while rubbing your head? And can you switch hands, with the left one on your head instead of the right one? Any new movement pattern seems awkward at first. But the brain soon learns to control the muscles and perform the action.

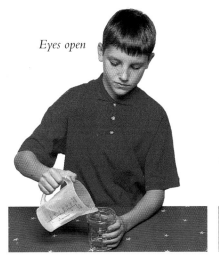

Eyes open

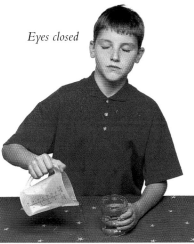

Eyes closed

The inner sense of position

You "feel" the positions of your body parts, especially muscles and joints, with your body's inner sense. You also watch your movements with your eyes, to guide them more accurately. Try pouring water from a jug in one hand to a glass in the other, with your eyes open. Easy! Now try with eyes closed. "Feel" your way using your inner sense. Splash … oh dear! Try again. Do you improve with practice?

Standing and falling

Balance is a continuous body process. The brain uses information from the eyes, skin, muscles, joints, and inner ears. It sends out instructions to the muscles to keep the body well-balanced. Stand still on two feet, close your eyes, lift one foot, and put your arms out at your sides. With less sense input, balance becomes more difficult.

Funny looks

Most of us use the same muscles every day, but, if you try to make a new face, you will be using muscles you don't normally use. Your face will feel funny and will look odd!

BIRTH AND BABIES

People are similar in body type to their parents because they inherit genes from them. Genes are found in body cells in the form of the chemical DNA. Half of them come from the mother, the other half from the father. They contain instructions for growth, development, and maintenance of the body. Each person has a unique set of genes, except for identical twins. The twins' genes are the same, so they look the same.

THE human body has parts and systems for many life processes, such as breathing, digestion, circulation, and excretion. It also has parts for reproduction, which involves the birth of more human beings. A woman has egg cells for reproduction in her ovaries. A man has sperm cells for reproduction in his testes. When a woman and a man have a baby together, her egg cell and his sperm cell have joined (fertilization) and developed into a baby. This development happens inside the female's body in a part called the uterus, or womb. After nine months of development, the baby is born. It emerges from the womb through the birth canal into the outside world. Over the years, the newborn grows and develops through the main stages of life, from baby, to toddler, to young child, to adolescent, to adult.

Sperm
Sperm cells look like microscopic tadpoles. Millions are made in the testes every day.

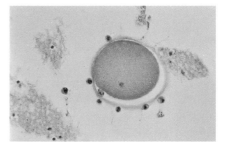

Eggs
Egg cells are huge compared to normal body cells. One egg ripens each month as part of the reproductive or menstrual cycle.

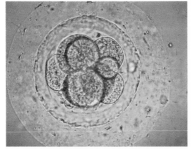

Fertilization
When an egg and sperm join, fertilization occurs. The fertilized egg becomes two cells, then four cells, then eight cells, and so on.

Developing baby

One week after fertilization, there is a microscopic ball of cells. They continue to multiply – into hundreds, then thousands, and millions – inside the mother's womb. Gradually, the ball of cells grows and changes shape. Two months after fertilization, it is a tiny baby, the size of a thumb. It already has a heart, muscles, nerves, and many other parts.

Umbilical cord

Muscular wall of uterus

Placenta

Cervix (opening or neck of uterus)

Birth canal

Inside the uterus

In the womb, it is warm, dark, and wet. The developing baby is in a pool of watery amniotic fluid. It cannot eat or breathe for itself. It receives all of its food and oxygen from the mother. The oxygen and nutrients pass from the mother's blood to the baby's blood through a dish-shaped part, called the placenta (afterbirth), in the wall of the uterus. The baby's blood flows back and forth between the placenta and its body through the umbilical cord. Nine months after fertilization, the baby is well-developed and ready to be born. The strong muscles in the uterine wall contract and push the baby along the birth canal. As the baby emerges into the world, it may cry, which helps it start breathing for itself.

First feeds

After birth, the baby breathes oxygen on its own. The mother feeds her baby on her breast milk, or other special milk. This milk contains all the nutrients that the baby needs in its first months outside the womb. The hours and days after birth are very important, as the mother and baby bond.

Growth

The baby grows into a young child. The body follows the instructions in its genes, but the child also is learning from others and developing into an individual with a personality, with likes, dislikes, wishes, and wants. He or she begins to crawl, stand, walk, talk, run, read, write, draw, make friends, go to school, and learn lessons … life is always busy!

GLOSSARY

adrenaline – a hormone that comes from the adrenal glands. It can make the heart pump faster when we are afraid or injured.

alveoli – microscopic pockets for air at the ends of the bronchioles in the lungs.

amniotic fluid – the watery substance that surrounds and protects a baby as it develops in the mother's womb.

anvil – a very small bone in the middle ear, shaped somewhat like a blacksmith's anvil.

atrium – the smaller of two chambers on each side of the heart from which blood flows, through a one-way valve, into the larger chamber below, where it is pumped out into the arteries.

bronchus – one of two main air tubes at the bottom of the windpipe that branch out into many smaller air tubes, called bronchioles.

cartilage – tough, elastic, slippery tissue in parts of the body, such as the joints, where it covers the bones for protection and smooth movement.

cerebellum – a large part of the brain that controls voluntary movements and controls balance.

cochlea – a space in the inner ear, shaped like a snail shell and filled with fluid, where sound vibrations are turned into nerve signals that go to the brain.

collagen – a body protein found in bones and skin that makes bones slightly flexible and keeps skin firm.

decibel – the unit of measure used to specify the volume (loudness) of a sound.

dentine – the bone-like tissue under the enamel of teeth.

dermis – the sensitive inner layer of skin beneath the epidermis (the tough, protective outer skin), which contains blood vessels, nerves, touch sensors, hair roots, and sweat glands.

enzyme – a protein produced by living cells that, along with acids in the digestive tract, breaks down the food we eat until it is small enough to pass through the lining of the digestive tract into the body.

esophagus – the first part of the digestive tract, a muscular tube that connects the throat to the stomach.

glottis – the opening between the vocal chords near the top of the windpipe through which air flows for normal breathing. It closes, almost completely, when speaking to allow air flowing past to vibrate the vocal chords.

keratin – the tough protein that is the main material in hair and fingernails and in the claws, hooves, and horns of certain animals.

melanin – a dark pigment in hair and skin which causes them to be different colors.

microscopic – too tiny to be seen without a microscope.

molecule – the smallest bit of something that still has all the same physical and chemical ingredients of the bigger object from which it came.

nephron – one of about a million microscopic filters in the outer layer of a kidney that removes waste matter from the blood.

neuron – a nerve cell with long, thin branches that connect to other nerve cells forming pathways throughout the body on which nerve signals travel to and through the brain.

pancreas – a gland that makes enzymes which break down food in the small intestine.

papillae – the small bumps on the top of a tongue that contain taste buds and help grip food.

peristalsis – the squeezing and pushing action of the muscles in the digestive tract that moves food along from the esophagus to the rectum.

pigment – a substance that gives hair and skin its color.

pulmonary – refers to things that affect the lungs, such as the pulmonary artery, which carries blood from the heart to the lungs, and pulmonary circulation, the process in which blood is pumped into the lungs to get more oxygen before it moves on to the body.

respiration – the process of breathing in and out to give the body oxygen.

septum – a thin piece of body tissue that divides the inside of the nose into two nostrils.

spirometer – a scientific instrument that measures the amount (volume) of air breathed in and out.

stirrup – one of three very small bones in the middle ear. (It is shaped much like a stirrup used in horseback riding.)

symmetrical – the condition in which an object is exactly the same shape and size, and has exactly the same features, on both of its sides.

systemic – something that affects the entire body, such as systemic circulation in which blood flows throughout the body delivering food and oxygen to body cells in the main body, head, arms, and legs.

ventricle – the larger of two chambers on each side of the heart that gets blood from the atrium above it and pumps it, on the left side, to the aorta and, on the right side, to the pulmonary artery.

villus – one of thousands of tiny, short, hairlike parts on the lining of the small intestine through which digested food is absorbed and delivered to the bloodstream.

visceral – refers to one of three main types of muscles in the body which perform their actions automatically rather than by the conscious control of the brain.

BOOKS

A-Maze-ing Human Body. John Berg (Readers Digest Young Families)

An Amazing Machine. Alan Parsons (Watts)

Body Facts. Anita Ganeri (EDC)

How Does A Cut Heal? Ask Isaac Asimov (series). Isaac Asimov (Gareth Stevens)

How Our Blood Circulates. Merce Parramon (Chelsea House)

How Our Senses Work. Jamie Ripoll (Chelsea House)

Human Anatomy in Full Color. John Green (Dover)

Human Body. Steve Parker (DK Publishing)

Human Body Systems (series). Alvin Silverstein, et al. (TFC Books)

Inside Story: The Latest News About Your Body. Mike Lambourne (Millbrook Press)

It's All in Your Head: A Guide to Understanding Your Brain and Boosting Your Brain Power. Susan L. Barrett (Free Spirit)

A Kid's Guide to the Brain. Sylvia Funston and Jay Ingram (Firefly Books, Ltd.)

The Living World. Record Breakers (series). David Lambert (Gareth Stevens)

Our Bodies. Under the Microscope (series). John Woodward (Gareth Stevens)

Professor I.Q. Explores the Brain. Seymour Simon (Boyds Mills Press)

Why Do People Come In Different Colors? Ask Isaac Asimov (series). Isaac Asimov (Gareth Stevens)

VIDEOS

All Systems Go. (AGC Educational Media)

The Bone Show. (Pyramid Media)

Mind Your Own Body: What's a Body? (PBS Video)

Story of the Blood Stream. (Pyramid Media)

WEB SITES

kidshealth.org/kid/

sln2.fi.edu/biosci/heart.html/

Some web sites stay current longer than others. For further web sites, use your search engines to locate the following topics: *blood, bones, digestion, heart, human body, nervous system, senses, and skeletal system.*

INDEX

PICTURE CREDITS

b=bottom, t=top, c=center, l=left, r=right

Biophoto Associates: pages 19tl, 22cr, 24cb and cr, 30tr, 37tl, 39c, 62r and b, 63tl. P. Gordon: page 36br. Alistair Hughes: page 10tl. Andrew Syred/Microscopix Photolibrary: pages 10br, 11tr, 37tl, 42tl, 51 inset, 56tl, 62l. Angela Hampton/ Reflections Photolibrary: page 63br; Jennie Woodcock/Reflections Photolibrary: pages 11cr, 24tl. Alfred Pasieka/Science Picture Library: pages 19ct, 28br; A. B. Dowsett/Science Picture Library: page 51t; John Reader/Science Picture Library: page 37tr. Tony Stone Images/David Madison: page 58tl; Tony Stone Images/Chris Harvey: page 63bl. Trip/K. Cardwell: page 9bl; Trip/A. M. Bazalik: page 23bl; Trip/R. Williamson: page 44tr. Zefa Pictures: pages 23bc, 28bl, 48tl.